SO, YOU'RE GETTING MARRIED

by

FRED SAHNER

Illustrated by

LENNIE PETERSON

CCC PUBLICATIONS

Published by

CCC Publications
9725 Lurline Avenue
Chatsworth, CA 91311

DEDICATION
To David and Lynn

Manufactured in the United States of America

Cover/Interior art by Lennie Peterson

Cover/Interior production by Oasis Graphics

ISBN: 1-57644-044-3

If your local U.S. bookstore is out of stock, copies of this book may be obtained by mailing check or money order for $5.95 per book (plus $2.75 to cover postage and handling) to:
CCC Publications; 9725 Lurline Avenue, Chatsworth, CA 91311

Pre-publication Edition – 9/97

INTRODUCTION

THIS BOOK WILL PUT THE 'HAPPY COUPLE' ON THE ROAD TO MARITAL BLISS. GATHERED HERE, IS ALL THE INFORMATION YOU WILL NEED FOR A SUCCESSFUL WEDDING AND A HAPPY MARRIAGE.

MARRIAGE HAS MANY ADVANTAGES, SUCH AS, SOMEONE ELSE TO SPLIT THE RENT WITH, A LOVED ONE TO MOVE HEAVY OBJECTS AND A DON JUAN TO PICK UP THE DRY CLEANING. YOU SHOULD ENTER THE MARRIAGE AS MOST OTHER COUPLES DO - WITH FINGERS CROSSED AND A BOTTLE OF ASPIRIN AT THE READY.

NOTHING IS AS MUCH FUN AS PLANNING A WEDDING, UNLESS YOU COUNT ROOT CANAL WORK. MARRIAGE IS THE ULTIMATE DATE, THE ONE IN WHICH THE GUY DOESN'T GO AWAY WHEN THE NIGHT'S OVER.

ONE SECRET TO A HAPPY MARRIAGE IS: DON'T GO TO BED ANGRY WITH EACH OTHER; STAY UP AND CONTINUE THE ARGUMENT UNTIL YOU WIN. WE'RE TALKING ABOUT BEING THE BOSS HERE, FOLKS.

ON THE 'BIG DAY', BE SURE TO REVEL IN THE SPOTLIGHT; ENJOY THE ATTENTION AND TAKE YOUR SHOES OFF EVERY CHANCE YOU GET.

FINALLY, AND MOST IMPORTANTLY, HAVE A GREAT WEDDING AND THE BEST MARRIAGE ANY TWO PEOPLE HAVE EVER HAD!

IMPORTANT WEDDING ADVICE

BE SURE TO OBTAIN A PROPER LICENSE

(YOU DON'T WANT TO LEARN AT THE LAST MINUTE, THAT YOUR LICENSE IS ONLY GOOD FOR OWNING A COCKER SPANIEL)

THE BAD NEWS IS... I CAN'T MARRY YOU. THE GOOD NEWS IS... YOU CAN SHOOT GEESE FOR THE NEXT MONTH!
JUSTICE OF THE PEACE

THE COMMON SENSE APPROACH TO PLANNING YOUR WEDDING

A. CAREFULLY DETERMINE YOUR BUDGET

B. SHOP LONG AND HARD FOR GOOD BUYS

C. IGNORE ITEMS 'A' AND 'B' AND SPEND LIKE THERE'S NO TOMORROW.

WE'RE ON A STRICT BUDGET... SO, OUR LIMIT IS ONLY **SIX** DANCING ELEPHANTS AT THE RECEPTION

TREASURED WEDDING RITUAL #1

ON THE WEDDING DAY, IT'S BAD LUCK FOR THE GROOM TO SEE THE BRIDE BEFORE THE CEREMONY.

(A TRADITION THAT SAVES MANY MARRIAGES)

A HARMONIOUS PRE-NUPTIAL AGREEMENT SHOULD BE LOVINGLY PREPARED,

PRIOR TO THE WEDDING.

THREE CRITICAL CLAUSES FOR A PRE-NUPTIAL AGREEMENT

1) FOR THE FIRST YEAR, NO ONE SAYS, "SEE, I TOLD YOU SO!!"

2) THERE WILL BE NO COMPLAINING ABOUT MOTHER-IN-LAWS FOR AT LEAST THE FIRST MONTH.

3) THE FIRST PERSON (HUSBAND OR WIFE) TO GAIN 50 POUNDS, MUST CUT BACK TO EIGHT BETWEEN-MEAL SNACKS A DAY.

HERE IT IS...
I GET THE BATHROOM FIRST
ON MONDAYS, WEDNESDAYS
AND FRIDAYS!

SUGGESTIONS FOR THE BRIDAL GIFT REGISTRY

WELL WISHERS SHOULD GIVE ITEMS REQUESTED BY THE NEWLYWEDS. THE TYPICAL GIFT LISTS ARE:

THE BRIDE'S REQUESTS	THE GROOM'S REQUESTS
CUTLERY	BEER COOLER
CHINA	VALUABLE BASEBALL CARDS
LINENS	MUD FLAPS
TOWELS	'DIE HARD 2' (THE VIDEO)
POTS & PANS	A 'BUD' TEE-SHIRT
QUILT	A 'DO IT YOURSELF' TATTOO KIT

HE'S UPSET WE DIDN'T GET A BELT SANDER

IMPORTANT WEDDING ATTIRE TIP #1

DON'T BUY A GOWN WITH AN EXTRA LONG TRAIN

(EITHER IT WON'T FIT INTO THE CHURCH OR GUESTS WILL BE BETTING ON WHEN YOUR TRAIN WILL ARRIVE)

NOW I KNOW WHY IT'S CALLED A "TRAIN"–
THE TAIL-END SHOULD BE ARRIVING IN AN HOUR!

IMPORTANT WEDDING ATTIRE TIP #2

DO NOT BUY A CHEAP VEIL

(YOU DON'T WANT TO LOOK LIKE YOU'RE EXPECTING AN ATTACK OF THE KILLER MOSQUITOES)

BURLAP

IMPORTANT WEDDING ATTIRE TIP #3

EIGHT HELPFUL LISTS OF WEDDING WEAR TO SUIT THE OCCASION

	FORMAL	SEMI-FORMAL	CASUAL
HEAD WEAR	TIARA	SMALL HAT	SUN VISOR
OPTIONAL	VEIL	HALF VEIL	DISHRAG
SHOES	HEELS	FLATS	FLIP FLOPS
TRAIN	80 FEET	6 FEET	BASEBALL CAP
CARRYING	BOUQUET	A ROSE	A WEED
DRESS STYLE	ROYAL	TRADITIONAL	FRONTIER
COLOR	WHITE	OFF WHITE	POLKA DOT
FABRIC	SATIN	RAYON	BURLAP

REMEMBER TO SAY "NO THANKS" WHEN THEY OFFER US PICTURES OF THIS

WHAT TO EXPECT AT YOUR BRIDAL SHOWER

- GIFTS OF NIGHT GOWNS THAT WOULD EMBARRASS A STRIPPER
- HEARING ENOUGH 'OOHs' AND 'AHHs' TO LAST YOU A LIFETIME
- HAVING PEOPLE SHOW UP, WHOSE SHOWER YOU AVOIDED
- RECEIVING THE SAME GIFT FROM TEN PEOPLE

I BET SHE'S GOING TO LOVE THIS BLENDER!

ADDRESSING THE WEDDING INVITATIONS

A HANDY GUIDE TO PROPER INVITATION ETIQUETTE

PERSON IS	ADDRESS INVITATION
RICH RELATIVE	DEAR EXTREMELY WONDERFUL PERSON
YOUR BOSS	DEAR EXTREMELY WONDERFUL PERSON
POOR RELATIVE	TO WHOM IT MAY CONCERN
STATE PRISONER	DEAR #1129-007A8
YOUR EX	DEAR STUPID
HIS EX	DEAR LOSER

IF SOMEONE IS IN THE MIDDLE OF A SEX CHANGE, DO I ADDRESS THEM AS "MR.", "MS." OR "TO **WHAT** IT MAY CONCERN"?

SHARING THE WEDDING RESPONSIBILITIES

YOU AND YOUR FUTURE SPOUSE ARE ABOUT TO BECOME A TEAM, A TEAM THAT MUST SHARE DUTIES AND RESPONSIBILITIES. THE WEDDING IS A GOOD PLACE TO SHOW HOW THE CHORES ARE DIVIDED.

- GROOM'S RESPONSIBILITIES: SHOWING UP FOR THE WEDDING
- BRIDE'S RESPONSIBILITIES: EVERYTHING ELSE

SOME MALE BEHAVIOR PATTERNS YOU MUST UNDERSTAND

WHEN HE'S UPSET	SITS IN FRONT OF TELEVISION, MUMBLING
WHEN HE'S THINKING	SITS IN FRONT OF TELEVISION AND SCRATCHES HIS HEAD
WHEN HE'S FEELING SEXY	SITS IN FRONT OF TELEVISION AND TURNS ON 'BAYWATCH'
WHEN HE'S TIRED	SITS IN FRONT OF TELEVISION, SNORING
WHEN HE'S HUNGRY	SITS IN FRONT OF TELEVISION WHINING FOR NACHOS

TREASURED WEDDING RITUAL #2

NOTHING MUST CHALLENGE THE BRIDE'S DAY IN THE SPOTLIGHT. TO INSURE THAT THE BRIDESMAIDS ARE OVERLOOKED, THEY MUST WEAR DRESSES SO UGLY THEY WOULD SCARE FREDDY KRUEGER.

SURE, SHE'S ALL DOLLED UP, WHILE WE LOOK ABOUT AS ATTRACTIVE AS MONTH-OLD DONUTS!

FAVORS FOR THE WEDDING GUESTS

STUCK FOR PARTY FAVOR IDEAS?

...WELL, HERE ARE A FEW POPULAR ITEMS.

1) SMALL GLASS VASE THAT CAN'T HOLD A SINGLE FLOWER.
(IDEAL FOR MEASURING LOCAL RAINFALL)

2) GOBLETS, WITH THE WEDDING DATE INSCRIBED.
(SUITABLE FOR STORING IN ATTIC)

3) MONOGRAMMED BOOKS OF MATCHES
(PREFERABLY NOT THE TRICK 'EXPLODING' KIND)

HOW NICE...
THE WEDDING IS
SPONSORED
BY
"MURPHY MUFFLERS"

THE GOLDEN RULE OF WEDDING ALBUMS

THE ALBUM MUST CONTAIN AT LEAST ONE PICTURE OF THE GROOM

OKAY, THAT'S THREE ROLLS OF YOU AND THE FLOWER... NOW, LET'S SHOOT A ROLL OF CLOSE-UPS OF YOUR HANDS

TREASURED WEDDING RITUAL #3

A WELL-MEANING RELATIVE WILL
EMBARRASS THE GROOM

SO, OUR LITTLE STINKY IS MARRIED!... FROM NOW ON I'LL HAVE TO CALL YOU **BIG** STINKY!

BASIC WEDDING WISDOM #1

PRE-MARRIAGE JITTERS ARE NORMAL. BUT, IF YOU DEVELOP FOUR FACIAL TICKS, HAVEN'T SLEPT IN A WEEK AND ARE DRINKING A QUART OF GIN A DAY...YOU MIGHT WANT TO SKIP THE CEREMONY AND GO DIRECTLY TO DEVIL'S ISLAND FOR A FUN WEEK-END.

RELAX, ARTIE... IT'S ONLY THE BIGGEST DECISION OF YOUR LIFE!

THE SEVEN WORST WEDDING GIFTS YOU COULD RECEIVE

1. A KNITTED TOASTER COVER
2. A BOOK COVER FOR THE T.V. GUIDE
3. A YEARS SUPPLY OF EAR WAX REMOVER
4. A SCALE THAT LOUDLY ANNOUNCES YOUR WEIGHT
5. A SET OF WHISKEY TUMBLERS FROM OPREYLAND
6. "HIS" AND "HERS" SNOOPY SLIPPERS
7. DINNER PLACEMATS WHICH DEPICT "CLOSE-UPS OF THE WORLD'S WORST DISEASES"

HEY! ONE AT A TIME!!

BASIC WEDDING WISDOM #2

EVERYONE SHOULD BE ON THEIR BEST BEHAVIOR, JUST IN CASE SOMEONE IS VIDEO TAPING THE CEREMONY.

SECRETS OF THE BACHELOR PARTY - EXPOSED

THE BACHELOR PARTY: A SOLEMN GATHERING OF MEN, INTENDED TO PREPARE THE GROOM FOR MARRIAGE AND OTHER GROWN-UP ACTIVITIES.
THE BACHELOR PARTY AGENDA:

1) A PROLONGED DISCUSSION OF MALE AND ESPECIALLY FEMALE ANATOMY.

2) TO ILLUSTRATE THE ANATOMY DISCUSSION, A FEMALE MAY BE BROUGHT IN. THIS "SPECIMEN" WILL DANCE WILDLY, SO THAT THE GROOM WILL APPRECIATE THE NIMBLE MOVEMENTS OF THE FEMALE FORM.

3) TO AVOID LOSING THEIR VOICES - LIQUID REFRESHMENTS WILL BE SERVED.

4) THE BODIES OF FORMERLY THIRSTY FRIENDS WILL BE ROLLED TO ONE SIDE OF THE ROOM.

5) HEART WARMING STORIES ARE RELATED ABOUT THE MATING HABITS OF HOMO SAPIENS.

6) FOOD WILL BE SERVED FROM THE ALL IMPORTANT '3 P' FOOD GROUP: PIZZA, PRETZELS AND POTATO CHIPS.

7) MALE BONDING REACHES A HIGH POINT WHEN THE GROOM IS THROWN NAKED INTO THE STREET, BY HIS FRIENDS.

8) RANDOM ARRESTS TAKE PLACE.

9) GROOM APPEARS FOR THE WEDDING, HAVING CONSUMED 84 ASPIRINS AND SIX BOTTLES OF PEPTO-BISMO.

MAKE SURE THE GROOM TAKES PART IN PLANNING THE BIG DAY...

HOWEVER, LETTING HIM PICK OUT WHICH BEER TO SERVE, IS ALL YOU CAN TRUST HIM WITH.

THINK I JUSS ABOUT GOT IT NARROWED DOWN

BASIC WEDDING WISDOM #3

IF THE FLOWER GIRL LOOKS TOO CUTE FOR WORDS, MAKE SURE YOU AIR BRUSH HER OUT OF THE PICTURES.

(HEY, IT'S THE BRIDE'S BIG DAY, NOT THE BRAT'S)

WHO TO INVITE TO THE WEDDING

1) ANYONE WITH MORE THAN $50.00 TO THEIR NAME.

2) YOUR BOSS. (BE SURE TO GET HIM LOADED SO YOU CAN TAKE INCRIMINATING PICTURES)

3) YOUR PARENTS. YOU NEED TO KEEP THEM HAPPY SO THEY WILL PAY FOR THE SHINDIG.

4) A GOOD FRIEND WHO WILL PROVIDE AN ALIBI IN CASE YOU DO SOMETHING ILLEGAL.

5) AN OLD FLAME, SO YOU CAN GLOAT.

HOW NICE, SOME OF YOUR RELATIVES EVEN WORE SHOES!

**BE SURE TO HAVE A
DOUBLE RING CEREMONY;
ONE RING FOR YOUR FINGER,
AND ONE FOR THE
GROOM'S NOSE.**

5 SIGNS YOU WILL HAVE IN-LAW TROUBLE

- YOUR MOTHER-IN-LAW PLANS TO JOIN YOU ON THE HONEYMOON
- YOU SAY "HELLO," AND YOUR FATHER-IN-LAW ASKS WHAT YOU MEAN BY THAT
- YOU EAT DINNER AT YOUR IN-LAWS, AND THEY CHARGE YOU FOR THE MEAL
- THE IN-LAWS DON'T USE YOUR NAME, BUT REFER TO YOU AS "HER!"
- YOUR MOTHER-IN-LAW ASKS HOW SOON WILL HER ROOM BE READY

I'M SO GLAD YOU'RE MARRIED... YOU KNOW WHAT THEY SAY, THREE CAN LIVE AS CHEAPLY AS ONE!

HOW TO TELL YOUR HUSBAND WANTS SEX

- HE SHOWERS FOR MORE THAN 8 SECONDS
- HE CONSULTS TV GUIDE, TO BE SURE THAT SEX WON'T INTERFERE WITH A GOOD SHOW
- HE SAYS EXTREMELY ROMANTIC THINGS, SUCH AS: "SO, ER, YOU WANNA DO IT, OR WHAT?"
- HE GIVES YOU HIS SEXY 'LOOK'........WHICH CONSISTS OF:

– HALF CLOSED EYES

– POUTY SMILE

– HANDS ON HIPS

(TRY NOT TO LAUGH WHEN HE STRIKES THIS POSE. HE THINKS HE LOOKS LIKE ELVIS, EVEN THOUGH HE REMINDS YOU OF UNCLE FESTER)

THEY WENT TO A COMMERCIAL BREAK... C'MON, WE GOT A FULL SIXTY SECONDS TO FOOL AROUND!

BASIC WEDDING WISDOM #4

SOME WEDDING TRADITIONS ARE BEST IGNORED

SOMETHING BORROWED??...I THOUGHT IT WAS SOMETHING STOLEN!

TREASURED WEDDING RITUAL #4

IT'S CUSTOMARY FOR THE MOTHER OF THE BRIDE TO CRY DURING THE WEDDING CEREMONY.

HOWEVER...

IF SHE THROWS A TANTRUM, REFUSES TO BREATHE OR ATTACKS THE GROOM WITH A SHARP INSTRUMENT – YOUR HUSBAND MAY NEED THE HELP OF THE 'FEDERAL GROOM PROTECTION PROGRAM'.

IF ANYONE KNOWS A REASON WHY THIS COUPLE SHOULD NOT BE... UH OH!!

4 ANNOYING WEDDING DAY EVENTS

1) ANYONE GARGLING DURING THE TOAST

2) THE BEST MAN ORGANIZING A BURPING CONTEST

3) THE BRIDE SAYS, "GOD HELP ME", AFTER SAYING, "I DO"

4) THE FLOWER GIRL TAKING A HALF HOUR TO GET DOWN THE AISLE

THERE'S NOTHING THEY CAN DO... IT'S HER NAP TIME

GUIDELINES FOR WRITING YOUR OWN WEDDING VOWS

1) NO VOWS – SO LOVEY-DOVEY THAT THE GUESTS ALL BECOME ILL

2) NO VOWS – THAT RHYME OR RAP

3) NO VOWS – INVOLVING A HUMAN SACRIFICE

4) NO VOWS – SHOULD TAKE LONGER TO READ THAN THE BIBLE

ZZZZ
ZZZ
ZZZZ
ZZZZ

BASIC WEDDING WISDOM #5

THE MOST COMMONLY ACCEPTED FORM OF MARRIAGE STILL INVOLVES TWO HUMANS. NO MATTER HOW MUCH YOU LOVE YOUR PET, THE FLEAS WOULD EVENTUALLY COME BETWEEN YOU.

DUTIES OF THE FATHER OF THE BRIDE

- SUPPLY THE MONEY NEEDED TO PULL THE WHOLE THING OFF
- STAY PLEASANT, EVEN WHILE BEING IGNORED
- BRING THE BRIDE FROM THE BACK OF THE CHURCH TO THE FRONT WITHOUT FALLING DOWN
- TO GIVE THE BRIDE AWAY WITHOUT DEMANDING A RECEIPT

DUTIES OF THE MOTHER OF THE BRIDE

- MUST SMILE UNTIL MIDNIGHT
- MUST PRETEND THE GROOM IS WORTHY OF HER DAUGHTER
- MUST HUG PEOPLE SHE DOESN'T EVEN LIKE
- MOST NOT CRITICIZE THE GROOM UNTIL AT LEAST THE FOLLOWING DAY

WELL, YOU TOLD MOM SHE COULD SUPPLY THE ENTERTAINMENT!

HOW TO HAVE AN INEXPENSIVE WEDDING

- GET MARRIED AT SUNRISE IN THE PARK
- LET THE GUESTS FORAGE FOR THEIR FOOD
- FORGET THE LIMO, AND HITCHHIKE TO THE CEREMONY
- PICK THE BRIDE'S BOUQUET OUT OF SOMEONE'S GARDEN
- PASS AROUND A CANTEEN OF WATER AND FORGET THE CHAMPAGNE

5 QUESTIONS THE BRIDE MUST ASK THE GROOM BEFORE THE WEDDING

1) DOES HE UNDERSTAND THAT YOU ONLY ENTER THE KITCHEN TO GET ICE CREAM FROM THE REFRIGERATOR?
2) WOULD HE ENTER A BLAZING BUILDING TO RESCUE YOUR NAIL POLISH?
3) DOES HE UNDERSTAND THAT WHILE YOU DON'T DO HOUSEWORK....YOU WILL BE SUPERVISING HIM, AS HE DOES THE CHORES?
4) DOES HE EXPECT YOU TO ACCOUNT FOR EVERY LITTLE THOUSAND DOLLARS YOU SPEND AT THE MALL?
5) WILL HE START EVERY MORNING BY ASKING YOU, "WHAT CAN I DO TO MAKE YOU HAPPY TODAY?"

ME AND ALICE SHARE ALL THE DECISIONS...
SHE MAKES THEM AND I CARRY THEM OUT

"I DO", ARE THE LAST WORDS SOME HUSBANDS EVER SAY

OKAY... THAT'S ENOUGH OUT OF YOU, CHARLIE!

TIPS FOR THE CONSIDERATE WEDDING GUEST

REMEMBER:
TAKE THE RICE OUT OF THE BOX
BEFORE YOU THROW IT!

*(AND IF TOSSING COOKED RICE,
AT LEAST TAKE IT OUT OF THE POT)*

5 WAYS TO MAKE YOUR NEW IN-LAWS LIKE YOU

1) COMPLIMENT THEM ON THE JOB THEY DID RAISING YOUR SPOUSE

2) DON'T SIT IN THEIR FAVORITE CHAIRS

3) ASK YOUR MOTHER-IN-LAW FOR THE RECIPE OF EVERY MEAL SHE SERVES YOU

4) NAME ALL YOUR CHILDREN AFTER THEM

5) TELL YOUR MOTHER-IN-LAW THAT HER BIRTHDAY SHOULD BE A NATIONAL HOLIDAY

TREASURED WEDDING RITUAL #5

EVERYONE MUST TELL THE BRIDE
SHE LOOKS RAVISHINGLY BEAUTIFUL

(HEY, WHAT'S A LITTLE EXAGGERATION AMONG FRIENDS?)

OKAY, IT'S YOUR TURN TO TELL ME HOW GORGEOUS I LOOK

IMPORTANT HELPFUL TIP #1

IF YOU'VE PUT OFF HAVING SEX UNTIL AFTER THE WEDDING - MAKE SURE THE LIMO HAS TINTED WINDOWS.

AT LEAST THEY WAITED UNTIL THEY GOT IN THE CAR

4 CHARACTERISTICS THE GROOM MUST POSSESS

1. ABILITY TO ANTICIPATE YOUR EVERY WISH

2 ABILITY TO SHOWER YOU WITH COMPLIMENTS

3. ABILITY TO PRAISE YOUR EVERY ACTION

4. ABILITY TO SERVE YOU BREAKFAST IN BED

4 CHARACTERISTICS THE BRIDE MUST HAVE

1. WILLINGNESS TO BE ADORED
2. WILLINGNESS TO LIVE WITH A LESSER HUMAN
3. WILLINGNESS TO BE 'THE BOSS'
4. WILLINGNESS TO BE SPOILED ROTTEN

IMPORTANT HELPFUL TIP #2

THE MARRIAGE IS OFF TO A BAD START IF THE GROOM BRINGS A DATE TO THE WEDDING.

DON'T WORRY...
THIS WILL ONLY
TAKE A MINUTE

IMPORTANT HELPFUL HINT #3

NO MATTER HOW MUCH THE BRIDE LOVES HER WEDDING DRESS, SHE MUST TAKE IT OFF SOMETIME.

DON'T MENTION THE WEDDING OR SHE'LL RE-ENACT THE ENTIRE DAY!

4 WEDDING DISASTERS

1. A VOLUPTUOUS STRIPPER SHOWS UP, CLAIMING TO BE THE GROOM'S WIFE.
2. THE GROOM BRINGS A PORTABLE TV TO THE CHURCH SO HE WON'T MISS THE 'BIG GAME'.
3. SOME SLOSHED UNCLE DIVES HEAD FIRST INTO THE WEDDING CAKE.
4. THE TRADITIONAL "YOU MAY NOW KISS THE BRIDE', TURNS INTO FULL, HOT BODY CONTACT.

YOU MAY NOW STOP KISSING THE BRIDE... PLEASE!

THE THREE TYPES OF WEDDINGS

	SMALL	MEDIUM	MONSTER
WEDDING PARTY	2	8	144
NUMBER OF GUESTS	3	88	71, 139
FLORAL TOUCH	1 ROSE	1 BOUQUET	HOLLAND
FOOD	RING DINGS	TUNA NOODLE ALA MODE	JULIA CHILDS COOKING A HAM
BEST MAN	A STRANGER	COUSIN IGGY	TOM CRUISE
MAID OF HONOR	THE SCHOOL CROSSING GUARD	VERA FROM BOB'S DINER	MISS AMERICA
HONEYMOON AT	A LOCAL MALL	UNCLE LARRY'S CABIN	PARIS & ROME

HOW TO TELL YOU DIDN'T MARRY WELL

- ONE OF YOUR NEW IN-LAWS IS IN THE WITNESS PROTECTION PROGRAM
- A TYPICAL QUESTION YOUR HUSBAND ASKS AT HIS JOB IS, "YOU WANT FRIES WITH THAT?"
- YOUR HUSBAND THINKS BEAVIS AND BUTT-HEAD BELONG ON 'MASTERPIECE THEATER'
- YOUR HUSBAND HAS A RESERVED PARKING SPACE AT THE UNEMPLOYMENT OFFICE

4 THINGS THE BEST MAN'S TOAST SHOULD OMIT

1. ANY MENTION OF PREVIOUS SPOUSES OR CURRENT GIRLFRIENDS
2. ANY MENTION THAT THE GROOM IS A CROSS DRESSER
3. ANY MENTION OF THE COUNTRY'S HIGH DIVORCE RATE
4. ANY MENTION THAT THE NEWLYWEDS ARE GOING TO A MARRIAGE COUNSELOR RIGHT AFTER THE RECEPTION

AND STEVE, SINCE THIS IS YOUR SEVENTH MARRIAGE, I THINK IT'S GONNA BE THE LUCKY ONE!
!

BASIC WEDDING WISDOM #6

NEWLYWEDS SHOULD TRY TO AT LEAST MAKE IT THROUGH DAY ONE, BEFORE FILING FOR DIVORCE.

GOD KNOWS I'VE TRIED LUCY, BUT THIS MARRIAGE JUST ISN'T WORKING OUT!

YOU KNOW WHO'S IN CHARGE, WHEN THE BRIDE FIGURINE HAS NUDGED THE GROOM FIGURINE OFF THE WEDDING CAKE.

<u>TREASURED WEDDING RITUAL #6</u>

THE FIRST DANCE IS A WONDERFULLY ROMANTIC MOMENT; THE BRIDE AND GROOM DANCING TO THEIR 'SPECIAL SONG'

ONE WARNING THOUGH....

NO MATTER HOW MUCH IT MAY MEAN TO YOU, PLEASE DON'T USE:

'THE BEER BARREL POLKA'

'YOUR CHEATING HEART'

'LONG, TALL SALLY'

'THE WILLIAM TELL OVERTURE'

OLD McDONALD
HAD A FARM
EE, EI, EE, EI
OH...

5 SIGNS THAT THE RECEPTION IS IN TROUBLE

1) THE BRIDE AND GROOM ARE ARM WRESTLING AT THE HEAD TABLE

2) THE GUESTS ARE SENDING OUT FOR PIZZA

3) THE BAND IS FOUR GUYS ON DRUMS AND ONE ON THE TUBA

4) THE WEDDING CAKE IS DECORATED WITH BROCCOLI, PICKLES AND CELERY

5) THE BEST MAN IS BODY SURFING ACROSS THE DANCE FLOOR

IT'S A BAD SIGN WHEN THE WAITERS ARE CARRYING STOMACH PUMPS!

THE MARRIAGE IS
OFF TO A BAD START
WHEN THE BRIDE AND GROOM
TAKE SEPARATE HONEYMOONS

TAXI
TAXI

<u>TREASURED WEDDING RITUALS #7</u>

WHAT A JOY IT IS, TO WATCH THE BRIDE
TOSS HER WEDDING BOUQUET,
TO THE HOPEFUL,
SINGLE WOMEN

(ALL OF WHOM SECRETLY HATE THE BRIDE FOR LANDING A GUY BEFORE THEY DID)

IMPORTANT HELPFUL TIP #4

THE RECEPTION IS PROBABLY NOT
A GOOD PLACE TO...
AUCTION OFF ANY CRUMMY WEDDING GIFTS

OKAY, WHO'LL START THE BIDDING ON THE "HIS AND HER MOPS"?

4 WISHES TO MAKE WHEN CUTTING THE CAKE

1. THAT YOU WILL ALWAYS LOVE (OR AT LEAST NOT COME TO HATE) YOUR SPOUSE

2. THAT YOU MAKE IT THROUGH THE DAY ON LESS THAN 16 VALUIMS

3. THAT YOU GET A DISHWASHER BEFORE HE GETS A HARLEY

4 THAT THIS IS THE LAST TIME YOU EVER HAVE TO CUT A WEDDING CAKE

THE MOST ENJOYABLE PART OF THE DAY...

WHEN YOU FINALLY GET TO TAKE YOUR SHOES OFF!

OH, THAT FEELS GREAT... I LOVE IT!
DON'T GET EXCITED... SHE JUST TOOK HER SHOES OFF

AN INDICATION THAT THE BRIDE'S FATHER SPENT A TON OF MONEY ON THE WEDDING:

HE'S AUCTIONING OFF HIS VITAL BODY PARTS

SPECIAL SALE PRICE
MY LIVER
$10,000
$5,000
$99.95
With ONIONS 50 cents EXTRA

10 ITEMS THE BRIDE WILL DEFINITELY WANT IN THE PRE-NUPTIAL AGREEMENT

1. THAT ALL PROBLEMS WILL BE WORKED OUT FAIRLY, EQUITABLY AND IN YOUR FAVOR.
2. THAT YOU HAVE FIRST DIBBS ON THE BATHROOM, UNLESS YOU ARE OUT OF THE COUNTRY, WHEN NATURE CALLS.
3. THAT YOU DO NOT COOK ON DAYS ENDING IN 'Y'.
4. THAT YOUR HUSBAND CAN WATCH ANY TV SHOW HE WANTS, UNLESS YOU SAY OTHERWISE.
5. THAT YOU WILL KEEP THE MAIL BOX CLEAN AND YOUR HUSBAND AGREES TO TAKE CARE OF THE REST OF THE HOUSE.
6. THAT YOUR MOTHER-IN-LAW'S VISITS MUST COINCIDE WITH THE ARRIVAL OF HALLEY'S COMET.
7. THAT YOUR HUSBAND CAN PICK A RESTAURANT, BUT IF YOU FROWN, HE WILL IMMEDIATELY REPEAL HIS DUMB IDEA.
8. THAT YOUR HUSBAND CAN BLOW $1.25 FROM EACH OF HIS PAYCHECKS, ON ANYTHING HE WANTS. (THE BALANCE HE FORKS OVER TO YOU)
9. THAT HIRING A MAID, COOK AND BUTLER IS THE TOP PRIORITY, SHOULD THE FAMILY HIT THE LOTTERY.
10. THAT SHOULD YOU TWO HAVE ANY DISAGREEMENTS, YOUR HUSBAND WILL RINSE HIS MOUTH OUT WITH CRAZY GLUE, UNTIL HE COMES TO HIS SENSES.

2 ITEMS THE GROOM WILL DEFINITELY WANT IN THE PRE-NUPTIAL AGREEMENT

1. THE RIGHT TO WATCH THE 'BIG GAMES' ON TELEVISION, WITHOUT BEING ASKED TO DO CHORES.

2. THE WIFE MUST UNDERSTAND THAT ALL GAMES ON TELEVISION ARE 'BIG GAMES'!

IMPORTANT HELPFUL TIP #5

THE PHOTOGRAPHER SHOULD TAKE LOTS OF PICTURES, BUT KEEP HIM ON A SHORT LEASH OR HE'LL SOON BE RUNNING THE WEDDING.

OKAY... NOW I WANT EVERYBODY LINED UP ACCORDING TO WEIGHT AND HAIR COLOR...
LET'S MOVE IT!!

POTENTIAL WEDDING NIGHT DISAPPOINTMENTS YOU DISCOVER........................

BRIDE LIKES	GROOM LIKES
THE RIGHT SIDE OF THE BED	THE RIGHT SIDE OF THE BED
FOREPLAY	NO PLAY
LIGHTS OFF	LIGHTS ON
SLEEPING IN A NIGHTGOWN	SLEEPING IN A NIGHTGOWN
MOZART	HEAVY METAL
LEISURELY BATHS	ONCE-A-MONTH SHOWERS
CNN	THE CARTOON CHANNEL

THAT REALLY WAS A COMB IN YOUR POCKET?

THE LAW OF FAMILY GATHERINGS

SOME FAMILY MEMBER IS BOUND TO BE TOTALLY EMBARRASSING AT THE RECEPTION...JUST HOPE IT'S ON THE OTHER SIDE OF THE FAMILY.

SORRY, ANNIE! BUT AFTER 40 BEERS I JUST GET A LITTLE SILLY

6 THINGS YOU WILL DISCOVER SHORTLY AFTER THE WEDDING

1. THAT ONE PERSON'S NECESSITIES, ARE ANOTHER'S LUXURIES
2. THAT GETTING MORE THAN YOUR SHARE OF THE BLANKET IS AN IMPORTANT 'POWER MOVE'
3. THAT 2 CAN LIVE AS CHEAPLY AS 10
4. THAT A HUSBAND SHOULD HAVE NO SAY IN PICKING OUT: FURNITURE, DRAPES, RUGS, PICTURES AND ESPECIALLY COLORS
5. THAT YOU EACH HAVE COMPLETELY DIFFERENT IDEAS OF WHAT CONSTITUTES A 'CLEAN BATHROOM'
6. THAT IT'S VIRTUALLY IMPOSSIBLE TO AGREE ON THERMOSTAT SETTINGS

OKAY, I'LL TURN UP THE HEAT, BUT DON'T YOU THINK YOU'RE OVER RE-ACTING?

HOW A HUSBAND CAN HELP WITH THE HOUSEWORK

A) HE CAN HIRE SOMEBODY TO DO THE CHORES

B) HE CAN KEEP OUT OF YOUR WAY

C) HE CAN LIVE IN THE GARAGE UNTIL HE PROVES HE'S HOUSEBROKEN

D) HE CAN WALK ON HIS HANDS TO KEEP HIS DIRTY SHOES OFF THE RUGS

E) HE CAN THROW OUT ALL THE CLOTHES HE HASN'T WORN SINCE PUBERTY

F) HE CAN TAKE YOU OUT TO DINNER EVERY NIGHT AND AVOID GETTING THE FAMILY DISHES DIRTY

IT WAS BARBARA'S IDEA... SHE'LL LET ME BACK IN THE HOUSE AFTER SPRING CLEANING
RALPH
SPOT

HOW A HUSBAND HELPS RAISE THE CHILDREN

A) HE WILL NOTIFY YOU WHEN THE BABY'S DIAPER IS FULL

B) HE WILL POINT OUT THE CHILDREN'S BAD HABITS, SO YOU CAN STRAIGHTEN THEM OUT

C) HE WILL TEACH THE CHILDREN HOW TO MAKE BARNYARD NOISES

D) HE WILL NOTIFY YOU WHEN THE BABY WAKES UP AT NIGHT

E) HE WILL PROVE TO THE CHILDREN THAT BEING AN ADULT ISN'T ALL THAT HARD

BEHAVE, OR YOU'LL TURN OUT JUST LIKE YOUR FATHER

FOUR WAYS TO KEEP LOVE ALIVE

1. COMPLIMENT YOUR SPOUSE:

example - "WOW, HONEY, YOU DON'T LOOK TOTALLY AWFUL IN THAT OUTFIT. I'M ALMOST WILLING TO BE SEEN WITH YOU IN PUBLIC."

2. SURPRISE YOUR PARTNER:

example - TELL HIM YOU WERE GOING TO BUY YOURSELF A $5,000 WATCH, BUT..."SURPRISE...I ONLY SPENT $4,000!"

3. SHOW AFFECTION:

example - KISS HIM, EVEN IF IT'S NOT YOUR ANNIVERSARY.

4. SMILE OFTEN:

example - IF HE DOESN'T DESERVE A SMILE, AT LEAST SNEER ATTRACTIVELY.

I ALWAYS OFFER JACK A CHOICE OF DINNERS...
EITHER **SEND** OUT OR **EAT** OUT

TITLES BY CCC PUBLICATIONS

Blank Books ($3.99)
SEX AFTER BABY
SEX AFTER 30
SEX AFTER 40
SEX AFTER 50

Retail $4.95 – $4.99
30 – DEAL WITH IT!
40 – DEAL WITH IT!
50 – DEAL WITH IT!
60 – DEAL WITH IT!
RETIRED – DEAL WITH IT!
"?" book
POSITIVELY PREGNANT
CAN SEX IMPROVE YOUR GOLF?
THE COMPLETE BOOGER BOOK
FLYING FUNNIES
MARITAL BLISS & OXYMORONS
THE VERY VERY SEXY ADULT DOT-TO-DOT BOOK
THE DEFINITIVE FART BOOK
THE COMPLETE WIMP'S GUIDE TO SEX
THE CAT OWNER'S SHAPE UP MANUAL
THE OFFICE FROM HELL
FITNESS FANATICS
YOUNGER MEN ARE BETTER THAN RETIN-A
BUT OSSIFER, IT'S NOT MY FAULT
YOU KNOW YOU'RE AN OLD FART WHEN...
1001 WAYS TO PROCRASTINATE
HORMONES FROM HELL II
SHARING THE ROAD WITH IDIOTS
THE GREATEST ANSWERING MACHINE MESSAGES
WHAT DO WE DO NOW??
HOW TO TALK YOU WAY OUT OF A TRAFFIC TICKET
THE BOTTOM HALF
LIFE'S MOST EMBARRASSING MOMENTS
HOW TO ENTERTAIN PEOPLE YOU HATE
YOUR GUIDE TO CORPORATE SURVIVAL
THE SUPERIOR PERSON'S GUIDE
GIFTING RIGHT
NO HANG-UPS (Volumes I, II & III – $3.95 ea.)
TOTALLY OUTRAGEOUS BUMPER-SNICKERS ($2.95)

Retail $5.95
SINGLE WOMEN VS. MARRIED WOMEN
TAKE A WOMAN'S WORD FOR IT
SEXY CROTCHWORD PUZZLES
SO, YOU'RE GETTING MARRIED
YOU KNOW HE'S A WOMANIZING SLIMEBALL WHEN...
GETTING OLD SUCKS
WHY GOD MAKES BALD GUYS
OH BABY!
PMS CRAZED: TOUCH ME AND I'LL KILL YOU!
OVER THE HILL – DEAL WITH IT!
WHY MEN ARE CLUELESS
THE BOOK OF WHITE TRASH
THE ART OF MOONING
GOLFAHOLICS
CRINKLED 'N' WRINKLED
SMART COMEBACKS FOR STUPID QUESTIONS
YIKES! IT'S ANOTHER BIRTHDAY
SEX IS A GAME
SEX AND YOUR STARS
SIGNS YOUR SEX LIFE IS DEAD
40 AND HOLDING YOUR OWN
50 AND HOLDING YOUR OWN
MALE BASHING: WOMEN'S FAVORITE PASTIME
THINGS YOU CAN DO WITH A USELESS MAN
MORE THINGS YOU CAN DO WITH A USELESS MAN
THE WORLD'S GREATEST PUT-DOWN LINES
LITTLE INSTRUCTION BOOK OF THE RICH & FAMOUS
WELCOME TO YOUR MIDLIFE CRISIS
GETTING EVEN WITH THE ANSWERING MACHINE
ARE YOU A SPORTS NUT?
MEN ARE PIGS / WOMEN ARE BITCHES
THE BETTER HALF
ARE WE DYSFUNCTIONAL YET?
TECHNOLOGY BYTES!
50 WAYS TO HUSTLE YOUR FRIENDS
HORMONES FROM HELL
HUSBANDS FROM HELL
KILLER BRAS & Other Hazards Of The 50's
IT'S BETTER TO BE OVER THE HILL THAN UNDER IT
HOW TO REALLY PARTY!!!
WORK SUCKS!
THE PEOPLE WATCHER'S FIELD GUIDE
THE ABSOLUTE LAST CHANCE DIET BOOK
FOR MEN ONLY (How To Survive Marriage)
THE UGLY TRUTH ABOUT MEN
NEVER A DULL CARD
THE LITTLE BOOK OF ROMANTIC LIES
THE LITTLE BOOK OF CORPORATE LIES ($6.95)
RED HOT MONOGAMY ($6.95)
LOVE DAT CAT ($6.95)
HOW TO SURVIVE A JEWISH MOTHER ($6.95)
WHY MEN DON'T HAVE A CLUE ($7.99)
LADIES, START YOUR ENGINES! ($7.99)

NO HANG-UPS – CASSETTES Retail $5.98
Vol. I: GENERAL MESSAGES (M or F)
Vol. II: BUSINESS MESSAGES (M or F)
Vol. III: 'R' RATED MESSAGES (M or F)
Vol. V: CELEBRI-TEASE